I0424896

Foreword

Helen D. Longstreet, b. April 20, 1863, grew up on her father's plantation near Carnesville, Georgia. She attended schools in Gainesville and later worked on her father's newspaper. General James Longstreet, of Confederate fame, was her childhood hero. It was when she was working as an assistant state librarian and he was conducting research for his book, From Manassas to Appomattox at the state Archives that their romance blossomed. They were married on September 8, 1897 in the Governor's mansion in Atlanta, Ga. They spent several blissful years together attending Washington functions and traveling around the country.

After Longstreet's death in 1904, she spent much of her time rehabilitating her husband's tarnished reputation. Among other things, she was a prolific writer, an avid environmentalist, a conservationalist, and, as an octogenarian, even ran for Governor in Georgia in 1950. She died May 3, 1962 at the ripe old age of 99.

This essay by Helen is a rebuttal to the charges by democratic Congressman Bell, who served on the Post Office and Post Roads Committee, that she ran a sloppy post office from 1904 to 1912. He further stated that she was not qualified to be a postmaster in Gainesville, Georgia because she was not a resident there. The charges, a result of partisan politics and spoilmanship, were all untrue.

Helen D. Longstreet

Trail of the Spoilsmen in the Gainesville, Ga., Post Office

By

Helen Dortch Longstreet, Postmaster under Roosevelt and Taft

To the Senate Committee on Post Offices and Post Roads:

Confirming the statement of my recent communication to your Committee, to the effect that President Harding had made known his intention to bestow upon me the commission of the Gainesville, Georgia, Post Office by Executive Order, President's Letter on the subject is submitted:

October 26, 1922,

My Dear Mrs. Eagan:
     The arrangement for the appointment of Mrs. Longstreet to the Gainesville, Georgia, post office has been made. I note, however that the protest is filed that Mrs. Longstreet has not been a patron of this office for something like eight years. Will you take the matter up

with Mrs. Longstreet and let me have information on this charge. If Mrs. Longstreet still claims her residence at Gainesville I think no protest will hold.

Very Truly Yours,

WARREN G. HARDING

Mrs. Katherine Livingston Eagan,
The Cairo, Washington, D. C.

I furnished the President a statement clearly establishing that Gainesville has been my legal residence since my marriage to General Longstreet most a quarter of a century ago. The charge of non-residence was dropped.

The President, shortly after his inauguration expressed his desire to recognize me by appointment commensurate with my business qualifications. My very partial friends in many sections had endorsed me for head of the proposed Public Welfare Department, in recognition of my nation wide campaign in the interest of establishing this Department. But the Department had not been created and the term of the Gainesville Postmaster was about to expire. I was not a candidate for this office. But in October the President conveyed to me through Mrs. Eagan that it would give him satisfaction to commission me in the Gainesville Post Office by executive order. I promptly replied that I would accept the commission with deep gratitude to him, whereupon the President arranged for my appointment as disclosed by his letter to Mrs. Eagan of October 26th.

"SELF DETERMINATION" IGNORED BY BELL

My friends expected my name to be sent to the Senate in accordance with the President's order, immediately upon the convening of Congress in extra session on November 20th. This did not occur and upon inquiry at Post Office Department, in three different conferences with the Postmaster General on November 25th, 27th and 29th , the Postmaster General stated to Mrs. Eagan that Congressman Bell who represents the Gainesville district, had made the charge that I would be objectionable to the patrons of the office as Postmaster and in consequence my life in Gainesville would be made most unhappy. I hold the charge an insult to me and a libel on the chivalrous people of Gainesville. Being detained at bedside of my aged Mother whose life hangs by slender thread I am unable to make a campaign among the patrons of the Gainesville office to refute Congressman Bell's cruel slander. But Mr. Bell's sudden interest in my happiness and his eager desire to contribute thereto by barring me from a position in which he wishes to retain a political lieutenant, is on a par with the love which Clemenceau and the French people feel for the prisoner of Dorn. Congressman Bell aided the spoilsmen of the Wilson administration in relieving me of the commission of the Office with full knowledge that the salary furnished my only means of support. In view of this fact I can't help wondering what might have happened to me if I had fallen into the clutches of one less concerned for my welfare than the Congressman now claims to be.

Thomas M. Bell

Congressman Bell, I am informed, favors something better for me than the Gainesville office, at a more lucrative salary, in Washington, where life would be pleasanter. "Self Determination," cardinal principle of the Fourteen Points evolved from a war fought out under the soulful slogan "To make the world safe for Democracy," is invoked in my case. I choose the Gainesville, Georgia post, cheerfully relinquishing to Bell's political protégé, the finer office, the handsomer salary, the more joyous days in the nation's capital.

Congressman Bell's Brothers Beneficiaries Of Mrs. Longstreet's Official Favor

When Bell and his associate spoilsmen succeeded in having me relieved of the commission of the Gainesville office under the Wilson administration, the Associated Press carried the report that Burleson stated my record in office had been inefficient. I appealed to the Senate which was then democratic, to investigate and vindicate my record. In a statement before the Senate Committee that made the investigation, I paid the following tribute to the efforts of the patrons of the Gainesville office to have me retained:

"During eight years when I exercised supreme power as the appointee of a republican President, I applied the merit test in the Gainesville office, and it chanced that every man appointed by me was a democrat. The choice positions in my office I gave to the brothers of the democratic member of congress from my District who sits within sound of my voice. The positions were Assistant Postmaster and Money Order Clerk. The money order clerk died in the service and the assistant postmaster is there today, classified through my efforts. I did not make the appointments for political reasons; but when I found that the best qualified men were democrats I lived up to the highest ideals of a republican form of government and I did not cripple the public service by turning them down for political reasons. During eight years of republican administration, the democrats of Gainesville were sheltered in the Gainesville Post Office behind a woman's petticoats. Did the patrons of the Gainesville office approve the war to displace me? No! No! The clean, the high-minded, the courageous men and women in that little city lined up behind me like a standing army. God bless them! More than five hundred telegrams and letters from the most representative men and women who patronize the Gainesville office (these were placed before Senate Committee) were filed with President Wilson during the month of April in behalf

Mrs. Longstreet Supported With Devotion Of "Old Guard" To Napoleon.

of my retention in office. No stronger letters were ever written in tribute to the efficiency record of a public officer. A petition for me, running into the thousands, including all classes and conditions of patronage of the Gainesville office, was rushed to President Wilson during the month of April. Telegrams to the cost of more than $100 were filed with President Wilson in my interest during the month of April. There would not be found two hundred patrons of the Gainesville office whom the combined efforts of the water power trust and the spoilsmen could have controlled against me. But it was not the intention of my friends, who made a brief campaign for me during a few days of the month of April, to do more than testify to my efficiency record and to establish irrefutably, that the interests of the postal service called for my retention in office. Delegations of both sexes implored President Wilson for an audience. They wished to come to Washington in my behalf. Since this hearing has been granted by your Committee, my people have communicated to me that they were ready to come here and appear before your Committee with me. But I thought that would be an unnecessary expense and that I would be able to do all the talking that should be done on this occasion. Oh, while I have the power to remember anything I shall remember the support given me by the lovable, high-hearted people of Gainesville, for whom I have worked for the past eight years; and if earth memories may pierce beyond the thin veil, I shall remember and be grateful through the endless lapses of eternity."

Disgraceful Condition Of Gainesville Office When Mrs. Longstreet Took Charge.

When President Roosevelt appointed me Postmaster at Gainesville, W. R. Keys, a Post office Inspector, was in charge, the postmaster having been removed for inefficiency. Inspector Keys told me that he had never, in an experience of more than twenty years in the service, seen a post office in the deplorable condition that the Gainesville office was in at that time. The office was the dirtiest place in Gainesville. It was an eyesore to the town. A lady could scarcely walk through the lobby without getting her skirts ruined. The

Albert S. Burleson

internal arrangement was a veritable old curiosity shop. When it became necessary to refer to important and valuable records, which are required to be kept with great care and accuracy, it was a question of days to find them, as they were all thrown together in a junk heap, in a dark loft in the rear of the main work room where they had been accumulating for some eight or ten years. There were several tons of coal, kindling wood, rags, etc., in one end of the work room. I sent for the

Mayor to ask permission to dump the miscellaneous collection on the side of the street until a storage place could be secured. Hon. Howard Thompson was Mayor, and he delegated Mr. W. E. Dozier as his representative Mr. Dozier promptly gave the desired permission, remarking that he wondered the conglomerated pile had not long ago produced spontaneous combustion and destroyed the building by fire. I go this much into discreditable detail merely to make clear the state of disorder and inefficiency which distinguished the Gainesville post office at the time I was placed in charge. For a long time the town had been entitled to City Delivery and the surrounding country to a wider extension of rural delivery, both of which I promptly gave. I extended rural service by routes and loop routes over a mountain territory untraversed by railroads, more extensive than some of the New England states; until the mail was brought to every farmer within the delivery of the Gainesville office. In September, 1905, following my appointment in November, 1904, Post Office Inspector Keys who was in charge when I was appointed, was sent to inspect our city service. I had been successful in having City Delivery installed about four months after I was appointed Postmaster. Post Office Inspectors do not often permit themselves to be interviewed, but the improvements wrought during the first ten months of my term so gratified Inspector Keys that he gave an interview to the *Gainesville Eagle* which was printed in the issue of September 7th, 1905, in which he said; regarding the rearrangements I had made and the general improvements:

"No Other Office In Country Equals It" Inspector's Tribute to Mrs. Longstreet's Record.

"It is excellent. I know no other office in the country of this grade which equals it. The entire arrangement is as near perfect as it could be made, it seems, under present conditions, and it shows evidence of unusual ability possessed by the Postmaster. The working room, the carrier department and the storage room, all show evidence of the greatest care in arrangement, while the entire office presents the neatness of a well kept residence. In the arrangement of files and records, a matter that often gives an Inspector much worry, the greatest of ingenuity is evidenced. The arrangement is such that any record or file of paper can be had at a moment's notice. It is as cozy and attractive as a lady's boudoir. Going into the Postmaster's private office is a revelation to the visitor in Gainesville. It is nicely carpeted and furnished, and suitable pictures adorn the walls, the most striking one of which is an autograph portrait presented to the Postmaster by American's greatest and most beloved son, Theodore Roosevelt. Gainesville has good reason to be proud of her Postmaster and the excellent administration she is giving."

Congressman Bell's Treacherous Memory

The above references are for the edification of your Committee and also for the purpose of refreshing

Congressman Bell's memory. The Congressman has been accustomed, according to rumor, to claiming that his brother, A. B. Bell, Assistant Postmaster, was entitled to the credit for the success of my administration. Mr. Bell's brother had been in the office about twelve years before my arrival and a considerable portion of the long period, as Assistant, during which he exercised almost unlimited power; a sufficient length of time, it would seem, to show what he could do. The office under the administration of the Congressman's brother, was in the condition above described, when I took charge. I am also reliably informed that Congressman Bell claims that the Gainesville office was in the classified service when I was appointed Postmaster and I therefore had no power to dismiss his brothers and ensuingly, he (the Congressman) owes me no debt of gratitude for retaining them. This claim firmly established the treacherousness of Congressman Bell's memory. The records of the Department will disclose that City Delivery was installed at the Gainesville, Georgia, office early in 1905, about four months after I was commissioned as Postmaster. Prior to the establishment of City Delivery, the office was unclassified and the appointing power of the postmaster over the clerical force, was unquestioned.

Generosity To Political Foes Tests Chivalry Of Woman's Heart

I found Congressman Bell's two brothers in the Gainesville office when I was appointed Postmaster by Roosevelt, as previously stated. The office not being classified at that time, I had it within my power to dismiss or retain the Bell brothers. Immediately following my appointment two petitions were presented me by the patrons of the office, one asking for the

George B. Cortelyou

removal of Congressman Bell's brothers; the other, asking for their retention. Following quickly on these petitions, and before I had been in the office a month, I received a personal letter from Postmaster General Wynne, transmitting charges against the Bell brothers. The charges were to the effect that they had been in a mob that broke into the Gainesville jail and murdered a white prisoner who was held on the charge of having killed their father. The Postmaster General intimated that I might find it advisable to remove the Bell brothers from the Gainesville office. I replied that I would investigate the charges and if found to be true, would dismiss them. I made the investigation and found that congressman Bell's brothers were not guilty and I took the position before the Post Office Department (under severe pressure from republican machinery of Georgia, to have the Bell brothers removed from the

Gainesville office) that I would resign the commission as Postmaster before I would dismiss any clerk under a false charge. I thereby saved to Congressman Bell's brother(s), not only their salaries but their reputations, as well. A prince was in the White House and I knew that T. R. would support me in honest administration. A few months later, Lester Bell, the money order clerk, died in the service. Congressman Bell's brother, A. B. Bell, was retained by me as Assistant Postmaster and when, under the regulations, Assistant Postmasters became eligible for classification, upon my recommendation he was placed in classified service. And he is today in the Gainesville Post Office the beneficiary of my official favor in the hour when my power was absolute.

Persecuted By Congressman Bell For Eight Years

During my administration as Postmaster at a time when both of Congressman Bell's brothers were on the payrolls of my office, the Congressman had my stepson, Randolph Longstreet, removed from the position of cotton statistician for Hall County, Georgia, and the Congressman's father-in-law, Judge Winburn, appointed to the position. I took steps to have Mr. Longstreet reinstated and this marked the beginning of serious friction between Congressman Bell and me. On this occasion, when Roosevelt was President and Cortelyou, Postmaster General, Congressman Bell sent me word that he was seriously thinking of having me removed from office. I made the playful rejoinder that I regarded him as a very great man and believed it might be within his power to have me removed as Postmaster at Gainesville, but there were two men he would have to get rid of before he could reach me, Roosevelt and Cortelyou.

Following my encounter with Congressman Bell about the reinstatement of Randolph Longstreet, the Congressman continued (as) my relentless enemy during the remainder of my administration and rendered aid in having me relieved of office by President Wilson.

At the end of my first term Congressman Bell sought to prevent my reappointment. Roosevelt answered by sending my name to Senate the First day it convened with the statement that he reappointed me on my record in office. My record was "Excellent", 100, the highest the Inspector's Division gives. Boise Penrose, Chairman of the Committee on Post Offices and Post Roads, moved for my immediate confirmation and I became the first American to be confirmed in office while the signature of the Executive was still moist upon the parchment transmitting the nomination.

Mrs. Longstreet First American To Be Confirmed Immediately Nomination Was Read To Senate

Of that great honor paid me by the American Senate, the Atlanta, Georgia, *Georgian*, of December 14th, 1908, said editorially, in part:

"It is a matter of State pride that in deference to a Georgia woman the time-honored traditions of the American Senate have been broken.

"The tribute to Mrs. Longstreet is unique. For never before in the two-century stretch of the senatorial records has an appointment been confirmed by the wearers of the toga while the signature of the executive was still moist upon the parchment. Usually twenty-four hours, at least, are allowed to intervene. But scarcely sixty minutes elapsed between the signing of the commission by the President and the confirmation of the appointment by the Senate. This chivalrous act on the part of the Upper House of Congress was not simply a dip of courtesy to the fair sex, nor was it a patriotic concession to the widow of General James Longstreet On the contrary, it was a well-merited recognition of the splendid record which this brilliant Georgia woman has achieved in the office of Postmaster at Gainesville during the past four years. Indeed, the simple fact is that, upon the list of commissioned officials who have served the United States in similar capacity, she ranks first and foremost; and the course adopted by the Senate in this gracious act of recognition, which defies all precedent, graciously completes and rounds the compliment of President Roosevelt in making the appointment."

My confirmation in this charming manner was accomplished with concurrence of Senators Bacon and Clay, noble Georgians, who were my life long friends.

Bell Threatens To Remove Mrs. Longstreet

Congressman Bell amused himself during my second term as Postmaster by sending me a cheerful threat, every little while, that he would have me removed as soon as a democratic President reached the White House. I would always reply jokingly, that I believed it possible for one to be a democrat and also a gentleman, and a democratic president, if he were, in fact, a gentleman, would have no fight on a Postmaster who had a good record like mine. One day a friend of mine said: "Why in the world, don't you get rid of Tom Bell's brother. I wouldn't let A. B. Bell stay in the office and be persecuted by Congressman Bell." I replied that I was striving, under tremendous provocation, to square with standards that had been set for me at my mother's knee, in the glamorous May time. A. B. Bell, Assistant Postmaster, was rendering efficient service and I would have no reason to dismiss him except in retaliation; and I felt that if I did a cowardly thing like that, it would prove me as mean as Congressman Bell himself.

Mrs. Longstreet' Record Vindicated By Democratic Senate

At the conclusion of an exhaustive investigation, made upon my request, the Democratic Senate Committee that conducted the hearing on my record in the Gainesville office, reported as follow:

"The subcommittee to which was referred the request of Mrs. Longstreet for a hearing before the Post Office and Post Roads Committee of the Senate as to her administration of the Post Office at Gainesville, Ga., and in connection with the confirmation of her successor, Mrs. Ham, respectfully make the follow report:

"From the evidence and testimonials filed with the Committee in regard to Mrs. Longstreet's administration of the office, the Committee finds that she was efficient, capable and satisfactory as Postmaster. The Committee finds no objection to Mrs. Ham who has been named as Postmaster, and therefore recommends her confirmation.

> Claude A. Swanson, Chairman
> James K. Vardaman
> Joseph L. Bristow
> Charles E. Townsend

At the conclusion of the hearing which occurred on May 19th, 1913, Senator Swanson, a gallant Virginia gentleman, who was Chairman of the Committee, said to me, "Mrs. Longstreet, if Burleson attacked your record in office he should be man enough to retract."

Georgia's "Grand Old Woman" Testifies Before Senate Committee In Behalf Of Mrs. Longstreet

Mrs. Felton, Georgia's "grand old lady," recently seated as Senator from Georgia, was at my side. She had come all the way from Georgia without solicitation, to appear before the Committee in my behalf. In an eloquent speech Mrs. Felton said, in part:

"Mrs. Longstreet, widow of that brilliant old soldier, is here without any legal advice and she did not know that I was coming. In fact I had no thought of it until I left home unexpectedly Saturday, but I will stand up for the truth. I am a living witness. There never was a better or a cleaner or a better prepared post office in the State of Georgia than Mrs. Longstreet has had. I have had occasion to visit the Gainesville Post Office. I have witnessed its perfect order. I have seen the pride she has had in it, and I want to say that it is one of the nicest places you ever saw in the State of Georgia, and I have seen many of them and it has been her work and her inspiration. I am more than satisfied that the rejection of Mrs. Longstreet is entirely owing to Political prejudice.

Rebecca L. Felton

Mrs. Longstreet was rejected because she expressed her gratitude to former President Roosevelt, who was a candidate in 1912, and defended him from some very unkind attacks in various places. It seems to me a very strange demand when a small postmastership in the mountains of Georgia can not be held in her grasp if she thanks her benefactor for the chance that he had given her to earn an honest living in her poverty, thus being expelled from her position, and I am glad to say she has been constant in continuing to express her gratitude and I honor her for it. What are we coming to in this country when free speech is thus throttled? What will become of this race if one has to crawl on ones

21

hands and knees to hold public office. I do not forget that a former Republican President graciously gave another post office to the widow of a deceased democratic governor down in the State of Georgia. He gave Mrs. Atkinson the Newnan Post Office in such a charming way that one could almost glimpse a political millennium, because no man in the United States has been

Alexander S. Clay

more severely denounced and derided in Georgia than this Republican President while her husband was a

Longstreet's Glorious Memory and Faithful Service Deserve Better Treatment.

powerful political factor in the State. He certainly bore no malice and I am glad she has it. She holds the office now and is going to hold it. She was not disturbed by Roosevelt's successor, and I feel now that this gracious attention to a democratic governor's widow has been thrown into bold relief, and the dismissal of Gen. Longstreet's widow brings additional pain and sadness to my heart. President Jackson was a mighty factor in national politics in his time, and he actually dismissed his cabinet because of supposed rudeness to his beloved Rachel. His southern chivalry and marital devotion

22

were pronounced and active, but remained, in these latter days for Confederate States' politicians to fling out of doors Gen. Longstreet's beloved widow upon the charity of her husband's war time opponents, and to mask this deed by a false accusation as to her conduct in the office.

Warren G. Harding

"In my old age and widowhood I protest against this late and unkind attack upon Mrs. Longstreet's management of her Postmastership. It is an insult added to injury, and I am satisfied the administration is going to realize the seriousness of this mistake. I have nothing to ask at anybody's hands, gentlemen, thank God, but their good will and their respect, but may my right hand forget its cunning, may my tongue cleave to the roof of my mouth before I refuse to say that General Longstreet and his glorious memory and his faithful service deserve better treatment at the hands of a Confederate representation."

Knightly Soul of Harding

I turned the Gainesville office over to my successor in a beautiful white marble building, in the construction of which during my second term, I served as Disbursing agent and Assistant to Superintendent of Construction. The office enjoyed the distinction given it by Post Office Inspectors of being the best conducted second grade office in the United States. In the last inspection which was made in the spring of 1913, just a few weeks before the name of my successor was sent to the Senate, the Inspector reported that the service of the office was so perfect he could offer no suggestions for its improvement. I was permitted to read this report when the Senate committee called upon Burleson for my record.

When President Harding, my most loyal and generous friend, for whom I cherish deep reverence, made known his intention to commission me in the Gainesville office by executive order, he but expressed the desire of a knightly soul to reinstate me in an office from which I was unfairly removed by the spoilsmen of the Wilson administration. With whom will the Senate Committee choose to fellowship, Warren G. Harding or Thomas M. Bell?

When the President's intention was conveyed to me in October, I had under way plans that I hoped would enable me to take my aged mother, who is critically ill, to the Pacific Coast. These plans were abandoned and I communicated to the President that I would have great Happiness in accepting the Gainesville office. The emoluments would enable me to take my old mother back to die in the land of her birth, amid familiar scenes, surrounded by the comforts to which she has been accustomed and cheered by old friends.

Chivalry Of The Pioneer Georgian

My ancestors came to Georgia with Oglethorpe, founder of the colony, and on the bluffs above Savannah they unfurled a white banner on which was inscribed: "Not for ourselves, but for others." Two of my Georgia ancestors were distinguished officers in the war for American Independence, a picturesque stretch of land in Franklin County, Georgia (on which I was born) being granted them for service in that war. Among the romantic traditions of my family is a legend preserved in *White's History*, that, in the early days of the colony, one of my ancestors surrendered his life (almost on the spot on which I was born) in a battle with hostile Cherokees, before he would strike down an Indian squaw. His chivalry is commended to spoilsman Bell. When internal strife shook the continent, my kinsmen from Georgia and the Carolinas were

Augustus O. Bacon

mustered into the First Corps of the army of Northern Virginia, and every battle field of the Civil War was sodden with their heroic blood under Dixie's flags. I hold the degree of A. B. from Brenau College in Gainesville, which I attended in early youth. Gainesville has been my home during the nearly quarter of a century since my marriage. General Longstreet's residence of fifty years and his burial place there make

25

the southern mountain town historic and a shrine for travelers from other sections who frequently stop by to visit his grave. American and southern to the core, I feel that I lead the list among the women of Georgia who have a right to live in Gainesville and fraternize with her citizenry.

Baseless Slander

When Gen. Longstreet became identified with the republican party following the civil war, political enemies formulated the charge that he did disobey orders at Gettysburg and lost the Confederate cause and for fifty years they sought to blacken his military fame. The same spirit speaks in Congressman Bell's charge that I would be objectionable to the people of Gainesville as

James Longstreet

Postmaster. I was in the editorial chair as editor of a newspaper in one of the mountain counties of Georgia before I was eighteen. From that day to this, I have never asked consideration on account of my sex and I do not now. But I confess that my weak hands hold no weapons with which to defend myself against the methods of Congressman Bell.

Brand The Defamer

I beg your committee to illustrate the chivalry that is the glory and beauty of our western civilization in joining in my appeal to President Harding to send my name to the Senate according to his original plan, that I may be given the opportunity to lift the stigma that Congressman Bell seeks to fix upon a nan that will live forever in American history. Let him come before your Committee and tell what I have done to make myself objectionable to the people of Gainesville. If his charge is true, brand me before Americans, if untrue in honor and justice, brand him.

INDEX

Atkinson, Susan C.
(Milton), 22
Bacon, Augustus O., 18
Bell
A. B., 13, 14, 16, 19
Lester, 16
Thomas M., 7, 8, 14,
16, 19, 24, 25, 26, 27
Brenau College, 25
Burleson, Albert S., 8, 24
City Delivery, 12
Clay, Alexander S., 18
Clemenceau, 7
Congressman Bell's
brothers, 15
Construction Federal
Building, 23
Cortelyou, George B., 16
cotton statistician, 16
disorder and inefficiency,
12
Dozier, W. E., 12
Eagan, Katherine L., 5, 6,
7
excellent rating in Post
Office, 13
First Corps, ANV, 25
Fourteen Points, 8
Gainesville jail murder,
15

Georgian newspaper, 17
Gettysburg, 26
Hall County, Georgia, 16
Harding, Warren G., 6,
24, 27
Helen Longstreet's
appointment, 18
Inspector's Division
Grading, 17
Jackson, Andrew, 22
Judge Winburn, 16
Keys, W. R., 11
Longstreet
James, 6, 18, 23, 25, 26
Randolph, 16
Widow Helen, 23
Longstreet threatens to
resign, 16
Money Order Clerk, 9
official favor, 16
Post Office and Post
Roads, 17
Postmaster at Gainesville,
17, 18
Prisoner of Dorn, 7
Public Welfare
Department, 6
Roosevelt, Theodore, 4, 5,
11, 13, 15, 16, 17, 18,
21, 22

Senate Committee on Post
    Offices, 9
spoilsmen, 7, 8, 10, 24
Swanson, Claude A., 20
Thompson, Howard, 12
threats to Helen
    Longstreet, 19
tribute to Mrs. Longstreet,
    18

Upper House of Congress,
    18
White's History of
    Georgia, 25
Wilson, Woodrow, 7, 8,
    9, 10, 17, 24
Wynne, Robert J., 15